The Vikings in Greenland: The History of the Norse Expeditions and Settlements across Greenland

By Charles River Editors

A 12th century depiction of Vikings

About the Author

Sean McLachlan spent many years working as an archaeologist in Europe, the Middle East, and the United States. Now a full-time writer, he's the author of many history books and novels, including *A Fine Likeness*, a ghost story set in the American Civil War. Feel free to visit him on his Amazon page and blog.

About Charles River Editors

Charles River Editors is a boutique digital publishing company, specializing in bringing history back to life with educational and engaging books on a wide range of topics. Keep up to date with our new and free offerings with this 5 second sign up on our weekly mailing list, and visit Our Kindle Author Page to see other recently published Kindle titles.

We make these books for you and always want to know our readers' opinions, so we encourage you to leave reviews and look forward to publishing new and exciting titles each week.

Introduction

Nicholas Roerich's *Guests from Overseas* **(1901)**

The Expansion of the Vikings

Over the centuries, the West has become fascinated by the Vikings, one of the most mysterious and interesting European civilizations. In addition to being perceived as a remarkably unique culture among its European counterparts, what's known and not known about the Vikings' accomplishments has added an intriguing aura to the historical narrative. Were they fierce and fearsome warriors? Were they the first Europeans to visit North America? It seems some of the legends are true, and some are just that, legend.

The commonly used term, Viking, for the trading and raiding peoples of Scandinavia, may have originated from Viken (the large bay leading to Oslo), or it may have come from the Old Scandinavian words *vikingr* (sea warrior) or *viking* (expedition over the sea). The people from the north were known in western Europe at the time as Northmen or Danes, in England as Danes or pagans and in Ireland as *Finngall* for those of Norwegian origin and *Dubgall* for those from Denmark. In the east, in Russia and in the Byzantine Empire, the Scandinavians were called *Vaeringar* or *Varyags* (Varangians) or *Rus'*, the latter perhaps derived from the name Roslagen, a province in Uppland in Sweden.

Like many civilizations of past millennia, the Vikings are remembered in popular culture more for the fantastical accounts of their history than for reality. The written records of the history of the Viking period, consisting mostly of Norse sagas, metaphoric poems called skalds and monastic chronicles, were written down well after the events they described and tended to be lurid accounts rife with hyperbole. Furthermore, the most scathing tales of Viking raids are contained in the histories of monastic communities which were targets of Norse rapacity. These chronicles speak of the heathen Viking depredations of monastic treasuries and the ferocious torture and killing of Christian monks. The colorful bloody tales were certainly based on more than grains of truth, but they were also purposefully augmented to inject drama into history. Similarly Norse sagas written down in the post-Viking Age fixed what had hitherto been flexible oral tradition. They were often slanted to legitimize a clan or leader's authority by emphasizing an ancestor's bravery and skill in pillaging opponent's communities.

As a result, the almost ubiquitous depiction of the Vikings as horn-helmeted, brutish, hairy giants who mercilessly marauded among the settlements of Northern Europe is based on an abundance of prejudicial historical writing by those who were on the receiving end of Viking depredations, and much of the popular picture of the Vikings is a result of the romantic imagination of novelists and artists. For example, there is neither historical nor archaeological evidence that the typically red haired, freckled Norsemen entered battle wearing a metal helmet decorated with horns. This headgear was an invention of the Swedish painter and illustrator Johan August Malmström (1829-1901), and his work was so widely disseminated in popular books that the image stuck. Today the imaginary Viking helmet is an almost mandatory costume accessory in productions of Wagner's opera *Der Ring des Nibelungen*, which is not about the Vikings at all. It seems the horned helmet evolved from an imaginary reinterpretation of genuine Viking images of a winged helmet that may have been worn by priests in Viking religious ceremonies.

However, the Vikings' reputation for ferocious seaborne attacks along the coasts of Northern Europe is no exaggeration. It is true that the Norsemen, who traded extensively throughout Europe, often increased the profits obtained from their nautical ventures through plunder, acquiring precious metals and slaves. Of course, the Vikings were not the only ones participating in this kind of income generation - between the 8th and the 11th centuries, European tribes, clans, kingdoms and monastic communities were quite adept at fighting with each other for the purpose of obtaining booty. The Vikings were simply more consistently successful than their contemporaries and thus became suitable symbols for the iniquity of the times.

The Norsemen were also medieval Europe's greatest explorers, moving across the North Atlantic to settle in Iceland, Greenland, and even North America. Their settlements in Greenland were perhaps the most impressive, given that the bleak and unforgiving land was mostly uninhabited when they first made it there. Greenland is huge, measuring almost 840,000 square miles (1.35 million square kilometers). The interior is uninhabitable glacier and mountain, but the periphery is cut by countless fjords that shelter the inhabitants from some of the worst of the winds. The fjords in the western part of the island, especially the southwestern part, are made more temperate by relatively warm sea currents and can support grass and a diverse amount of wildlife. Even so, winters are harsh even in the southern latitudes, and ice clogs the northern reaches for much of the year.

Remote, and subject to long winters during which pack ice would cut it off from the rest of the world, Greenland seemed an unlikely place to found a colony. In fact, Greenland was only circumnavigated in the early 20th century, and many of its further reaches were unmapped until the modern day. Nonetheless, the Norse managed to live there for about 450 years among some of their most remote outposts, and Greenland would maintain strong ties to the rest of Europe.

The Vikings in Greenland: The History of the Norse Expeditions and Settlements across Greenland looks at the history of the Vikings' activities in Greenland, and how they affected subsequent exploration and colonization. Along with pictures depicting important people, places, and events, you will learn about the Vikings in Greenland like never before.

Historical Sources

The mention of the word "Viking" brings to mind a clear image. Though the Viking Age took place such a long time ago, the Viking culture is still one that's very much alive today in contemporary art, music, films, and our imagination. People all over the world instantly associate the word Viking with a tall, broad, muscular warrior, a long beard and hair, an axe in one hand, and the typical, round, wooden shield in the other. On top of a Viking's head is, of course, a horned helmet.

This image of the Viking can be found in tales and portraits over a thousand years after their real existence. One detail that seems to pass most people by is that they never actually wore horned helmets. In archaeological excavations, only one helmet has been found with decorative horns from the period. Vikings most likely fought with no helmets at all. People also mainly associate the Vikings with raiding, pillaging, raping, violent behavior, and committing unspeakable acts of cruelty, like the practice of blood eagle and drinking wine or mead from human skulls. Again, these images derive from mistranslations, exaggerations, and sources written by questionable witnesses at a much later time; in reality, the Vikings were mostly farmers and traders, and women were held in high regard in their culture.

The period referred to as the Viking Age took place roughly between 750-1050, and therefore there are not many available, surviving sources to shed a clear light on the Vikings' complex image. The written stories and contemporaneous manuscripts blend reality with myth. Though many of the characters surely existed, historians can only distinguish what actually did happen during certain important events of Viking history with difficulty. When studying written medieval history, it is of utmost importance to have a critical eye to the stories of witnesses and to read between the lines. What is not being said or what is being hinted at in an elaborate or insinuating way often plays a crucial role in revealing the truth behind a story.

Many of the sagas are also written in a very free poetic style with no set grammatical order. Therefore, the field of historical research contains a myriad of scholars interpreting sources in radically different ways. This is where two important factors will contribute to clear the mystery of what and who the Vikings were. Firstly, interdisciplinary research needs to be done to bring forth a full image of Viking culture, utilizing history, archaeology, literature, linguistics, numismatics, zoology, botany, geology, and many other disciplines. When viewing the Vikings from all of these perspectives, it is easier to define a specific Viking culture, find out why they were so different from other tribes, and why they had such a strong impact on Europe in the High Middle Age, an influence still very much visible today. The second important factor to keep in mind when considering, in particular, the archaeological finds, is that what has survived through the millennia does not necessarily represent defining objects of the era. The tools and accessories made of the strongest materials–swords, axes, and weapons–needed to be more enduring than many household objects, for natural reasons. That doesn't necessarily mean the Vikings were more violent and warring than any other contemporaneous culture, nor does it indicate they did not spend time on other more peaceful activities. It simply means the weapons used were made of steel such that they would last a thousand years, even buried at the bottom of a river.

The Middle Ages brought conflicts, wars, and violence of all sorts across Europe, and it should go without saying that it was not just the Vikings who raided and pillaged defenseless peasants. While studying the written sources, it is important to note that most of the surviving material was written by the invaded peoples, notably monks, priests, and scholars who were victims of Viking aggressors. These sources are highly biased, leaving out most of the details surrounding the visitor's sudden arrival. By leaving out the details, the writers simply had to state that a bishop had been slain by the Vikings, but not whether he had been killed in battle initiated by himself or his king, or if he had been cut down while peacefully praying. The reader is left to assume the pious bishop had been assaulted performing a holy sacrament, enhancing the ferocious image of the Vikings while exaggerating the differences between the brutal heathens and the righteous Christians. Religion played a pivotal role in the conflict between Western European kingdoms and the Northerners.

Another factor to keep in mind when dealing with contemporaneous sources is the loyalty the writers showed their kings. Charlemagne, for example, had been considered–and still is today– the father of modern Europe, uniting large territories and different tribes under one rule and one religion. The cruelties he committed while doing so is hardly mentioned, and today most people forget his purging of the Saxons, which was nothing short of an attempted genocide.

The image of Charlemagne had been produced by his subjects, endorsing him as a great and just king, chosen by God himself to unite Europe. This image is still alive today in popular science in the same way people still associate the Vikings with beards, a thirst for blood and the horned helmets which they never wore. Both of these images were originally produced by the biased witnesses, and there was no mention of Vikings being, first and foremost, traders and farmers, rather than warriors. The picture of the barbaric north is no longer valid as it had been created on the ideological grounds that European Christian culture was superior to the hedonistic Scandinavian one.

When studying the Viking Age or reading material produced on the subject, it is also important to remember that most information relates to the upper-classes, whose activities and deeds have been written down. Lower classes had no way of telling their story to future generations, but it's fair to assume the people in the northern and southern Scandinavian countryside lived completely different lives compared to citizens of the great trade centers of Hedeby or Birka. Moreover, there are more foreign sources than domestic ones found in Scandinavia, to the extent that when it comes to shedding light on events taking place in Norway, Denmark, and Sweden, there are only a few reliable written records. The skaldic poems, written from 1200-1400, are such stories kept alive through the centuries by wandering poets and storytellers. The main writer and transcriber of these poems was the Icelandic skald Snorri Sturluson, and his work, *Heimskringla*, is one of the most important collections of writing regarding the Viking Age. In it, the author argues for the authenticity of the poems by stating the nature of the poems doesn't allow for any changes or distortions. The verse's strict metrical rules leave no room for improvisation or any additional, made up information about the reality they portrayed. As long as they are sensibly interpreted, Sturluson claimed the *Heimskringla* was the most accurate testimony regarding the Viking Age, even though it was written down some 200 years later.

There are a few more collections of texts regarding life in Scandinavia that have survived through the millennia, though they contain errors, myths, stylish improvements, and chronological mistakes. Danish scholar Saxo Grammaticus and his German colleague, Adam of Bremen, produced two of the most vivid and lengthy descriptions of Scandinavia's population in the Viking Age, valuable when illustrating the impact the Viking expansion had on Europe. The scattered sources - sagas, runes, archaeological finds, foreign witnesses, laws, and codes - together shape an image of what life might have looked like for Scandinavians in the Viking Age. Since Scandinavia was not a literal culture in itself, very few sources from the actual time survive, and it's impossible to know the inner-thoughts or beliefs of individual Scandinavians during the Viking Age. The only things they left behind are runestones and inscriptions, usually in memory of someone in the family.

I. Berig's picture of a runestone in Sweden

Roberto Fortuna's picture of a 10th century runestone in Denmark

As for the Vikings themselves, they wrote trivial messages and letters to one another, albeit mainly on wood, which is why these have been lost to the centuries. Another problem when studying the Viking Age is the evolution of language; certain words in Scandinavian could have had different regional meanings, and their semantic meanings have probably changed through the centuries.

Despite all this, the Viking Age is the first Scandinavian era documented in texts and scriptures. In conjunction with archaeological discoveries of runestones, weapons, graves, and settlements, it's possible to at least fill in some blanks when it comes to the story of Scandinavian Vikings.

The Reasons for the Vikings' Future Expansion

Although most Vikings were farmers in the 8th century, initial expeditions carried out by earls, kings, and chieftains created an influx of wealth, ideas, and goods, which played a large role in creating modern Scandinavia. These trips were motivated by a number of push-factors and pull-factors, some of them revealed quite recently, and it is clear the conditions in Scandinavia motivated a number of young men to travel and seek glory across the seas.

There are a number of theories regarding the actual causes of the Viking Age. In the same way historians consider other sudden increases in the migration of people, they usually divide the arguments into push-factors and pull-factors. Push-factors are reasons to leave a place, while pull-factors are reasons to go to a specific place. The sudden Viking expansion has been previously explained using mainly pull-factors, such as the fact European villages, churches, and monasteries being easy and lucrative targets to plunder. However, after locating and making correct use of Scandinavian-written sources, it is now evident that many of the reasons for Viking expansion can also be explained as push-factors.

Some theories focus on the fact that Scandinavia had seen a slight increase in population, and that scarcity of food was one of the factors pushing people out across the ocean. This is, however, not enough to explain the Viking phenomena, and the small increase in population was important to the size of Viking bands, not to their actual existence.

What caused the Viking expansion to change from peaceful trading to violent raiding is better explained by interconnected factors pushing and pulling the Vikings across the oceans. Many scholars choose a cultural explanation, triggered by greater economic growth and the influx of wealth.

All of Europe had already expanded trade networks over the centuries leading up to the Viking Age, and many communities started reaping the benefits of these lucrative connections across the continent. During the 8th century, it was not only Christian countries but also Scandinavia that experienced rapid economic growth due to these trade networks. The small, established kingdoms around the continent and larger courts of Frankish and British kings used exclusive goods to manifest their power and might. They both dressed in and decorated their halls with exquisite furs, amber, walrus ivory, and other exotic materials, as well as adorning their loyals with expensive gifts. These networks of gift-giving and the need to show off riches and wealth to instigate the image of a powerful leader triggered a large expansion of trade with the northerners.

As the small networks of trade routes grew rapidly, Scandinavia was perfectly situated to take advantage of the flow of goods from the far north and east, south toward Western Europe. This increased demand for valuables during the 8th century gave birth to several new trading stations around the Scandinavian coastlines, and soon, it was not just the European chieftains and petty kings gaining power, wealth, and influence, but the Scandinavian leaders as well. By controlling the trade and ports with taxes, chieftains could grow in influence even though they owned small portions of land or no land at all. This sparked a small shift from loose farming communities to stronger, centralized towns and cities, where more people gathered in a smaller area, which transformed the power of the chieftains to include more citizens but less land.

The change taking place in the port cities had a profound impact on the government and leadership of Viking society. With more accumulated riches in the family, more people were attracted to contain the power leading to that lifestyle. The heirs of prosperous chieftains suddenly took much more interest in following in their father's footsteps than before. Previously, the sons of chieftains had, upon their deaths, split the land between them and continued with the farming of it. Now, the centralization of power and the smaller portions of land on which to farm gave rise to conflict between the heirs of the deceased chieftains. During the Viking Age, there was no set order of succession between brothers, giving each of them the right to claim the chiefdom. This naturally gave rise to a stretch of arguments which often spilled over into duels or battles between brothers, each of them supported by subsets of families and allies. The conflicts ended with the losing side being exiled, not just from the chiefdom but in some cases, also from the whole of Scandinavia.

These exiles were not the end for the princes though, as the Viking Age would come to prove. Though society was hierarchical, it was not static, and in many cases, these lost sons of the dead chieftains took the exile as an opportunity to travel, plunder, gather riches, and in some cases even return home with a great band of loyal followers to claim the lost throne.

The first acts of piracy or Viking raids were conducted within the realm of the Baltic Sea, against ships packed with valuable cargo, traveling from the north or east toward western Europe. They were, in fact, conducted by Scandinavians against Scandinavians, some of them men who had been exiled and were seeking revenge and fast booty. Indeed, the economic motives are probably the most important push-factors and the reason behind why the raids were so violent. Plundering proved more efficient than actually conducting trade. It is believed they changed their incentive from trading to raiding within a decade. The men who joined the exiled on their trips across the ocean also saw the chance to improve their living conditions faster than they could at home. This long chain of events is considered to be the most prominent push-factor behind the Viking Age.

There are also a couple of correlating circumstances facilitating the Vikings' expansion and success. The art of shipbuilding and the increase in iron production were two of these facilitating circumstances. It is hard to ascertain the reasons for the increase in iron production, but it led to the production of a greater number of weapons. They were not necessarily of better quality than those used in Europe, as had been previously concluded, but the sheer amount of them allowed a growing number of ordinary people the chance to learn how to handle them. As a result, when the northerners decided to take up arms instead of trading with the Europeans, the correlation between increased weapon production and practicing the wielding of weapons soon made the Vikings deadlier fighters than many tribes on the continent.

Vic Iarg's picture of a display of Viking swords

The other factor can be credited to the Viking ships. Scandinavia had long had a tradition of sailing, and their ships had particular characteristics making them easier to navigate in narrow and shallow waters like the fjords. By the start of the Viking Age, the northerners had just begun to combine their ships with the use of sails adopted from old Roman constructions. The Vikings became seafaring experts defining the era, giving rise to their legend. These two facilitators coincided with the push-factor of new societal changes, allowing the Viking expansion to make a strong impact over quite a short period of time.

Viking Ship, Viking Ship Museum, Oslo. Photo by Grzegorz Wysocki

In 1867 a dig in southeast Norway revealed a vessel dating back to about 900, and 13 years later another one was unearthed. In the latter burial, apparently for a man who had been murdered, the collection of interred objects and animals was gigantic. Buried with the man was a ship, a dozen horses, six dogs, a peacock, five beds, three small boats and shields, as well as other objects apparently deemed necessities of life for him.

In 1904 an even more spectacular find was made in a burial mound at Slagen in Norway, where the Oseberg ship was uncovered. This ship, the burial place of two women, one of whom was a slave, was carefully preserved and transported to Bygdøy, near Oslo, where it was reconstructed and put on display with the two other Norwegian vessels.

Oseberg Ship

The Oseberg ship, dated through dendrochronology (tree rings) to 820, is 70 feet in length with a beam of 17 feet. It is a clinker built boat, meaning the hull, consisting of the keel, stem and stern, were attached with iron nails to 12 overlapping oak planks (lap-strake) on each side of the hull. Then the stabilizing ribs, twarts and inner keel were inserted. This kind of construction is opposite to the more common procedure of laying down the keel and attaching the ribs before attaching the hull planking.

The course of the Oseberg ship was controlled by a rudder mounted on the starboard side of the stern, and it was powered by 30 rowers who manned oars made of pine. The effort required to set the Oseberg vessel in the burial mound indicates just how important the ship burial was in Viking society. The vessel would have been dragged from the sea and moved some distance on rollers up to the site of the mound, where it was loaded with the necessities of life for the deceased woman in the netherworld, such as knives, pots, beds, woolen blankets and quilts and her female slave. The burial also included a carved wagon, three sledges and a saddle, as well as dogs, oxen and horses. Archaeologists think the elaborate burial process would have taken about four months.

The clinker built Viking ship was strong and flexible, and it was caulked with yarns of wool. The thwarts, which maintained the rigidity of the hull, also served as seats for the rowers who were the only means of power for early Viking ships. In the period around 800 the sail was introduced and it became the most important means of power for Viking vessels and one which they learned to manage with remarkable dexterity.

Later Viking vessels have been found not in burial mounds but as wrecks. Among these ships was a long ship or war vessel found in Hedeby harbor, Denmark that was built in about 985 and was damaged and sunk about 25 years later. This ship was about 100 feet in length, with a beam of 8 feet, and was propelled by 60 oars and a large square sail. Since it had a height of only 4 feet amidships, it is assumed that it was for use in the protected seas of the coastal Baltic. There were also long ships that were more suitable to long open-sea voyages, and one of these was discovered underwater in the harbor Roskilde in Denmark. This particular vessel was about 100 feet in length and was built near Dublin in 1042. Another vessel from Roskilde is, on the basis of the surviving parts of the keel, estimated to have been an impressive 120 feet in length. Both of these ships had a depth amidships that was sufficient to allow the vessels to deal with the high seas of the Atlantic.

At the same time as they were perfecting the building of long ships, the Vikings constructed a number of specialized cargo ships that could be operated by a small crew. These ships had a few oars for maneuvering in confined waters like rivers and had shallow draughts, but they could still carry tons of freight. One of the five ships excavated at Skuldelev in Denmark, which measured 50 feet in length, could carry as much as 24 tons of freight. By sailing a reconstruction of this vessel, which dates back to about 1039 and is known as Skuldelev 1, it has been determined that the crew would have numbered between five and seven. The development of efficient trading vessels by the Vikings was probably due to the increased need for low cost consumer goods at home, as Scandinavian society became more stratified and the need to provide cargo service between Scandinavia and the far-flung Viking settlements grew.

Skuldelev Ship 2

The Vikings navigated their ships using "dead-reckoning", a method of establishing latitude by means of a sun-shadow board. A disc with a central pin that could be adjusted for the time of year was floated in a pan of water, and the sun at noon would cast a shadow on the disc that was marked for the correct latitude. The bearing could be adjusted depending on relationship of the shadow to the marking. This simple means of navigation was only infrequently relied upon as the Vikings tended to proceed on their voyages in legs hopping from island to island. Further in the Baltic and North Atlantic, the legs of the voyages were of short duration. A Viking ship could travel from Denmark to Scotland or Norway to the Shetlands in about 24 hours. From the Shetlands the Vikings sailed on to Ireland past the Orkneys and the Isle of Man or traversed the open north Atlantic to the Faroes on to Iceland and eventually further to Greenland and North America.

Thanks to their ships, the Scandinavian people traded with a number of regions all over Europe, and the 8th century saw many small trading posts scattered along the coasts. The purchasing power of the north made for a direct trade between Scandinavia and the rest, opening up for the possibilities of exporting their own raw materials and crafts. The most common things to trade in Scandinavia were slaves and furs, typical for the region, but the further north a fur came from, the more luxurious it was considered. This benefited the northern traders, soon hunting and conducting trade with nomads and tribes from the far north to be able to sell in Europe. Furs of white polar bears were held in great esteem and some of the Norwegian kings claimed these as a tribute by the northern Sami people, while some hunted them themselves. Otter, bear, reindeer and marten were other types of furs adorning the Viking traders with riches.

This also made the Viking Age traders travel further and further north and east in search of more exquisite and special types of fur. This took them all the way to the deep interiors of Russia, where many remnants of Viking settlements have been found.

It is also likely that the era saw an increase in trade of different foods. Instead of only eating what was grown locally, the Scandinavian population started consuming food made by others, and a lot of it came from far away. In the same vein, there are examples of Viking clothes made of silk or exotic fur, and they had jewels made of certain stones, leading historians to infer that these things also were traded. By the 10th century, it was more common to trade with crafted everyday goods, like combs and shoes, due to the influx of wealth that made it possible for more people to buy instead of making these things.

All metal items, except those made of iron, were important, and many blades made by mail came from the Frankish Empire, though they were really not supposed to sell weapons to their enemies. Salt, mercury, led, amber, walnut shells, glass, pottery and wine were some of the exotic goods coming into Scandinavia from the south, but intricate and decorative vessels, beads and crystals also came all the way from the Orient or Russia.

For their part, the products coming out of Scandinavia were mainly animal products, like skins and furs, walnut tusks and whale bones, but the slave trade was also prominent, both within Scandinavia and for the traders traveling to the continent. Records tell of, among others, Ottar and Wulfstan, two traders who sailed between Birka, Hedeby and England, and their journeys have been recorded on both sides of the sea. Another route led across the Baltic Sea, to a region in Latvia called Semigallia. From there local merchants transported the goods up along the river Dvina, which would likely require another type of ship. This was a common pattern of trade around Europe, where the Scandinavian merchants only sailed the coast lines and there sold their goods in bulk, bought new products and sailed back to the port towns of Scandinavia.

The Viking Age trade networks required many middlemen to connect distant lands with each other. The local trade and the rise of craftsmanship gave life to the towns and larger market centers, creating tighter bonds between the different territories. The Viking expeditions' large amounts of silver and gold coming into Scandinavia, attracted some interest from prominent merchants from faraway lands, like Spanish-Arabs, Saxons, Frisians and Slavs who left traces of goods as well as customs in the north. More than 800 Viking Age Arab silver coins have been found on Gotland, present day Sweden, indicating the popularity of these coins. Needless to say, very few sailors or merchants made the journey directly between the Arab Caliphate and Scandinavia, but there are some records from Arabs taking the journey. In most cases these coins likely traded hands a great many times, all the way throughout Europe on their way north.

More English silver coins have been found in Scandinavia than in England itself, also demonstrating the wealth of the Vikings during this era, provided both by skill in trade but perhaps mainly by the Vikings' ability to extort the English in search for riches. Wealthy Vikings could acquire plenty of silver from around the world, by trade, plunder, bribes, gift giving, or tributes, and pirates also started frequenting the northern seas, putting pressure on the local kings and chiefs to increase the protection of ships carrying goods into their ports. The protection was often provided by interdependent groups and communities that volunteered to do so. This created an essential trust between traders from different backgrounds, giving way to shared cultural norms and similar economic structures being developed in different places.

The tumultuous 9th century, during which trade was replaced with raiding to a great extent, weakened the Carolingian Empire, thus requiring stronger maintenance and control over the ports. Therefore, a number of the small trade stations were abolished during the most expansionist and violent period of the Viking raids. This period is when cities like Kaupung, Hedeby, Åhus, Lund and Birka came to flourish, and the trade patterns of both Scandinavia and the rest of Europe went through large changes during the 200 years of the Vikings' expeditions. The unity of the Scandinavian tribes made local warring impossible and made the northerners go elsewhere in search of lands to loot and pillage. By the end of the Viking Age, these cities had already started to decline thanks in part to the Russian principality around Kiev. The Russian king put a halt to the trade route connecting the Islamic caliphate and the Byzantine Empire with

Scandinavia and claimed many of the riches and goods for himself, directly affecting the life and prosperity of the Scandinavian trade centers.

Though the Viking Age is mainly remembered as a period of violence, and mainly portrayed as such, the Vikings' overall impact was actually positive. The trade they brought stimulated the economies of Western Europe, which had grinded to a halt with the fall of the Roman Empire. The victims of the raids surely had the right to complain, but there are, very accurately in this case, two sides to that coin.

Traveling across the North Atlantic

In the two centuries between 800 and 1000, the Norse expanded across the North Atlantic. Starting in the Shetland and Orkney Islands off the north coast of Scotland, they spread north and west to the Faroe Islands, Iceland, Greenland, and as far as Canada and more temperate parts in North America.

The Orkney and Shetland Islands were settled in the late 8th century and used as a base for raiding expeditions into Scotland. Norse tradition states that they first arrived in the Faroes around 825, but the archaeological record starts several generations later, with little hard evidence for early 9th century settlement. One explanation for this anomaly is that coastal erosion, which is rapid in this harsh environment, has taken away the earliest sites. There is some evidence that the Norse weren't the first people to get as far as the Faroe Islands. Some archaeologists have found evidence that grain was cultivated around 600, indicating that early Celtic monks may have lived in the area, something supported by somewhat vague literary evidence. These finds, however, are controversial and not accepted by many archaeologists. After 1100, there was an expansion of fishing in the North Atlantic on the Faroe, Shetland, and Orkney islands, and commercial fisheries appeared and boatloads of salted fish were sold for export all across northern Europe. All three of these island chains became an integral part of the northern trade routes.

The traditional settlement date of Iceland, circa 874, is more concrete. As with the Faroes, there is some evidence that Celtic monks may have gotten there first. An early site at Herjolfsdalur on the Westman Islands off the south coast indicates occupation in the seventh century. These Celtic monks, known by the name *papar*, are a persistent legend in the early sources, but there is no irrefutable evidence for them and the Herjolfsdalur site remains controversial.

Regardless of whether they were first or not, the Norse soon made Iceland entirely their own. Within a generation, much of the land had been taken up by stock farming, and people were already wondering what may lie further to the west.

The first Norse landing on Greenland was, according to the sagas, by Erik the Red in 982. Erik was an important figure from a respected family, but he had to flee Norway after he killed someone. Settling in Iceland, he married, had a son named Leif, and worked a farm, but he soon got into trouble with his neighbors after once again committing murder. After that, he was outlawed.

Since he couldn't go back to Norway, Erik headed west, looking for a place where he could live in peace. Eventually, he sailed with a small following and ended up somewhere on the southwestern coast of Greenland. They found uninhabited fjords, good fishing, and land that could be used for limited grazing. They did not meet any native peoples, who at that time lived further north. It was only during the Little Ice Age, which started in the late 13th century, that the natives began to migrate southwards to escape the colder temperatures and hunt the increased number of sea mammals found off the coast there.

According to Ari Thorgilsson in *Íslendingabók*, Erik "called it Greenland, and said the people would be more eager to go there if it had an attractive name. They found there human habitations, both in the eastern and western parts of the country, and fragments of skin boats and stone implements, from which it can be concluded that the people who had been there before were of the same kind as those who inhabit Vinland and whom the Greenlanders call Skrælingjar ["weaklings"]. He began colonizing the country fourteen or fifteen winters before Christianity came to Iceland [985 or 986] according to what a man who had gone there with Erik the Red told Thorkell Gellison in Greenland."

If this account is accurate, it suggests that some native people had lived in southern Greenland sometime before the Norse settlement. Thorkell was Ari's uncle, so Ari was getting this information from a source close to the events.

A few years after his initial landfall, Erik returned with 14 ships and several hundred colonists. While "Greenland" was obviously a grandiose and not entirely accurate description of the land, it was fertile enough along the southern third of its western coast, and grass was plentiful enough during the short summers to support cows, sheep, and goats. Hunting was excellent, with seals, walruses, whales, hares, wolves, bears, caribou, and reindeer being the main targets. There was no grain or fruit, however, and precious few vegetables.

Erik's son Leif left Greenland and spent some time at the court of King Olaf Tryggvason of Norway (ruled 995-1000). He returned around the year 1001 on the king's orders to bring Christianity to the distant colonies. Leif brought with him a priest, but Erik, a staunch pagan, was not pleased, calling the priest "a trickster." Nonetheless, Leif had the priest proclaim the new faith in the name of King Olaf. Erik's wife Thjódhild quickly converted and built a small church on their farm. The old pagan himself eventually converted late in life.

Thanks to these early efforts, the Viking settlements in Greenland were established, and they took on the distinction of being the westernmost Christian settlements in the world.

Life in Greenland

The Vikings clustered in two main settlements, which may bring up images of towns and villages, but this was not the case in Greenland, where the settlements were clusters of stock farms along the most hospitable of the fjords. Some farms were quite isolated.

The larger one was called *Eystribyggð* ("Eastern settlement"), which despite its name was on the southwestern shore close to the southern tip of Greenland. The *Vestribyggð* ("Western settlement") was located about 400 miles to the north near what is now Nuuk, the capital of modern Greenland. Both of these settlements are attested to in the sagas, while a third settlement not mentioned in the annals has been found just north of *Eystribyggð* and has been dubbed *Miðbyggð* ("Middle settlement"). It's the smallest and most scattered of the three.

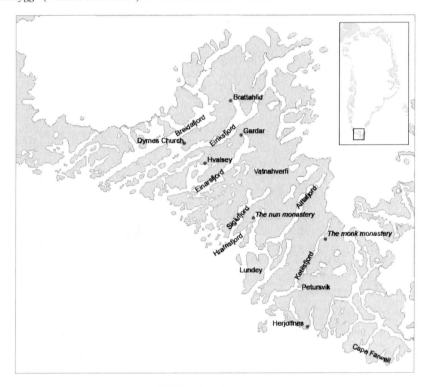

A map of Viking locations on Greenland

Scattered farms and fishing stations have been found in the lands between the three settlements and further afield, leaving historians to wonder if a fourth settlement may yet appear. Greenland is a vast place, with harsh weather that doesn't allow for a very long window in the year for archaeological excavations, so it's still possible that the history of Viking activities in Greenland may change radically with new discoveries.

The Eastern Settlement was founded on the best lands by Erik the Red in the 980s, while the Western Settlement, while in a much harder climate for stock farming, had better hunting and fishing. It was also considerably closer to the northern hunting grounds, where the Norsemen hunted walrus to tap into the lucrative ivory market, and it lay along the currents and winds that could bring voyagers to North America.

Like Iceland, Greenland was an independent proto-democracy with its own Althing, or parliament, which voted to accept Christianity. It also took measures to request a bishop. In 1261, Greenland became a crown dependency of Norway. It is unclear how big the population was, but it is clear that it steadily rose during the first century of colonization. Estimates of the peak population range from 1,500 to the improbably high figure of 10,000. A reasonable estimate seems to be no more than 5,000 at the colony's height in the 13th century.

As those numbers suggest, the size of the population in Greenland has been a matter of lengthy debate. While all agree, both from the textual and archaeological evidence, that the Eastern Settlement was considerably larger than the Western Settlement, perhaps three times as big, and the Middle Settlement was smaller than both, it is unclear just how many people were living in these areas at any one time. Many Norse farms have been located, but it's difficult to estimate the population based on these because it is unknown just how many farms remain to be discovered. Moreover, the Norse probably used the shieling system, meaning they moved their livestock to another area for part of the season to avoid overgrazing. This is a common practice in marginal areas, and it means each family may have had multiple farm sites.

It is assumed that the initial wave of immigration numbered at least 500 people in order to be genetically sustainable over time, and that there was a small yet steady immigration for a couple of more generations. Using this model, the population would grow steadily until it began to reach the land's carrying capacity and level out by the year 1200.

When discussing the farms in Greenland, it's important to remember that no crops were grown in the harsh climate, though the first generation may have made the attempt, as they did in the early, warmer years in Iceland. If they did, they no doubt tried to grow barley, the hardiest of the grains, but even in the warmer weather the Norse enjoyed in the first centuries of settlement, no farming would have been reliable. Thus, the farms were given over to raising cattle and sheep that grazed on the available grass, which was similar to Viking settlements in Iceland, where agriculture was limited in the warmer period and died out altogether in the later, colder times. *The King's Mirror* from the 13th century said the Greenlanders had "never seen bread," and for those people who had been born in Greenland and lived there all their lives, this was probably true, other than the communion wafers that would have been in use in the churches.

As with the rest of the Norse world, land was the key to social status. Those who had the biggest farms, the best land, and largest herds were considered the most respectable. Fishing and hunting were always secondary. This cultural trait explains why the Vikings never adopted the Thule (pre-Inuit) way of life, which was much better suited to the land. The Vikings simply did not want to be nomadic hunters.

Ultimately, this limited their adaptability, and it also led to the erosion of the soil. It is unclear how much erosion affected the long-term viability of the settlements, but many researchers believe it helped contribute to their eventual decline.

An analysis of animal bones found in various Greenland farms also found some interesting variations. The richer farms had proportionally more cattle, reflecting their more extensive pastures and probably also the urge to show off status by having a large herd of cattle, something the Norse admired wherever they settled. Smaller farms had mostly sheep and goats, and the poorest farms had few domesticated animals at all. The largest proportion of the bones found on these poorer sites were from seal. Seal blubber was used for lighting, and while the Norse preferred not to eat seal, the poorest people had to make do with what they could get.

The richest farms were, of course, in the best areas, the sheltered valley bottoms of the inner fjords. The poorer farms were closer to the coast, or higher up the slopes, stuck on inferior land that could not support nearly as many domesticated animals. The sparser plant cover in these areas was more vulnerable to overgrazing and erosion, and indeed it appears that many spots were made useless after a time.

Numerous farms have been excavated, but the most fruitful excavation to date has been of a well-preserved farm in the Western Settlement that was occupied from the first half of the 11th century to perhaps the end of the 15th century, covering nearly the entire Norse Period. The farm is located near Nipaitsoq, only six miles from the edge of Greenland's ice cap. It has been called The Farm Beneath the Sand due to being covered by layers of sand from a meandering river. During the Viking Age, it was on dry land, but the course of the river changed and layer upon layer of sand was deposited over the farm site, helping to preserve it. During the excavation, the archaeologists had to struggle with floodwaters from the river flowing nearby.

The first thing that became apparent to the archaeologists was the large amount of wood used to build the farmhouse, and a lot of the wood lacked any of the shipworm holes found on driftwood. This indicated the wood had been imported. The site went through several phases but remained more or less of the same character, consisting of a large house of several rooms in which most of the activity took place in a main room built around a long hearth. The building had stone foundations with walls made of a mixture of wood and turf. These walls ranged from 20-40 inches thick and would have provided ample protection from the elements. The roof was not well preserved, but it appears to have been a pitched latticework of branches covered by a thin layer of turf. The floor was covered with brushwood.

Animals were kept in rooms attached to the house, with paved floors (to facilitate cleaning) and stall partitions. Many medieval homes incorporated sheds for livestock into the structure, which kept the livestock safe under the watchful eye of the owners and contributed to the heating of the building. The preservation of the site, buried as it was under sand in a permafrost layer, was such that these stables still smelled of manure, and those on the team who had grown up on farms could distinguish the smell of cow manure from that of sheep and goats.

Indeed, bones of all three animals were found at the site, as well as those of horses and dogs. The sheep and goats were far more common, which made sense since they were more suitable to the marginal grazing Greenland offered. Wild game such as hare, seal, and caribou were also found, and whale vertebrae appear to have been used as chairs and tables. Polar bears, arctic wolf, and walrus were probably also hunted when the Vikings went to the northern hunting grounds far up the western coast.

What's remarkable was how few fish bones were found. While fish bones decay easily, this site was remarkably well preserved and was further proof that the Vikings in Greenland largely ignored the bounty all around them and preferred to live as stock farmers.

The site was rich in artifacts, including a room in which was found the remains of an upright loom, complete with loom weights and spindle whorls. Wooden bowls, a wooden cross, horn spoons, combs made of bones, and even a wooden door made of Siberian driftwood were found.

Artifacts often showed a clever use of what materials were at hand. For example, a spade was made of a wooden handle and the shoulder blade of a whale. Shallow soapstone bowls were used as lamps for burning whale and seal blubber, which gave off a long-lasting if not particularly bright light. More elaborate items included a carved box with a lid and a panel of wood carved in an Early Gothic floral design.

Three examples of Runic writing were found at the farm on three different objects bearing the names Thor, Bardur, and Bjork. The third name, the only female one, was found on the bottom of the carved box lid mentioned above.

One unusual find was a bracelet made of braided hair from a fair-haired person. This practice of making bracelets out of a loved one's hair was common in Scandinavia right up to the modern day.

Of equal interest is what was not found. No valuable items were among the finds, and most of the tools and other objects had already broken and been discarded. Also, no large objects other than the loom were left behind when the inhabitants finally abandoned The Farm Beneath the Sand. The exodus was orderly and unrushed, so there was room in the boat for everything important.

Remains from the hearth had some charcoal. It's surprising that wood, being so scarce, would have been burned, but perhaps this was driftwood that was unsuitable for being carved into something more useful. Dried animal manure was the main fuel.

While the excavations at The Farm Beneath the Sand have told researchers a great deal about life in Greenland, they have also created a tough question. Radiocarbon dating indicates that the farm lasted until almost 1500, about 150 years after the Western Settlement was supposedly abandoned. Indeed, a written Norse account discusses how in the middle of the 14th century a cleric named Ivar Bardarson was sent by the people of the Eastern Settlement to the Western Settlement because they hadn't heard from them for many years. Ivar didn't find any people, only abandoned buildings and stray farm animals. Are the Carbon 14 dates wrong, or did the Western Settlement hang on for a lot longer than previously supposed? Only further excavations might provide an answer.

One detail from the final phase of The Farm Beneath the Sand corroborated Ivar's account. The stalls had a lot more dung in them than normal, as if animals had been left there, perhaps with the door open so they could graze, and the animals returned to the stalls at night for shelter. Perhaps when the last residents left, they didn't have room for all the animals and had to leave some behind to fend for themselves, thinking they could go collect them later. In one room in the final phase of the farm, a goat was killed when the wall collapsed on it. This evocative scene of a crumbling, abandoned farm killing its last resident serves as a fitting obituary of sorts for the Western Settlement.

While this is the most spectacular excavation in Greenland in recent years, there have been many other excavations of farms, churches, and graveyards that have unearthed a great deal of information that helps paint a picture of the medieval way of life. Like in all medieval communities, life was dictated by the seasons, so the brief summer was a time of frantic activity. It was the only practical time to sail to the northern hunting grounds, and it was also the time that ships came to and from Greenland, probably late in the season in order to take advantage of the ivory and walrus skins gathered from the northern hunting expeditions.

Livestock would fill themselves on the grasses and would be at their most fruitful. Each animal would be milked as much as possible in order to make cheese and *skyr*, a type of yogurt, to be stored for the long winter months when the animals' milk production went down. In late summer, the farmers would also harvest hay to keep their animals through the winter. There would also be hunts for seabirds, whose colonies would be at their peak size at this time. The bones of two species, murre and guillemot, are the most commonly found in Norse sites. These two species go through a life cycle that leaves them flightless, and thus easily collected, in late summer.

With the onset of winter, the animals would be brought into their pens to wait out the season. At this time, the caribou, which would have been grazing along the coast in summer, migrated inland and provided the inhabitants another chance to hunt. They would hide behind lines of cairns, first constructed by the Paleo-Eskimo long before the settlement era, to drive the caribou into killing zones. Hunting dogs would help with the drive, and the animals would be shot with crossbows or stabbed with spears. The entire community would participate, and the meat would be shared.

During winter, the people would take care of the animals in their pens, make tools, and rest. Gaming pieces show they had some diversions, and no doubt the people told sagas like their Icelandic brethren. There is little evidence of winter hunting, as the climate was rough and most of the migratory animals had left.

Late winter and early spring were, like elsewhere, the leanest months. Stocks would have run low, especially if there had been a poor season the year before. If the Vikings had adopted harpoon technology, they could have gone ice hunting for ring seals, a major food source for the Thule people during the winter months. Instead, relief only came for the Vikings in the spring when the harp seals returned to the shoreline areas to give birth. Like with the caribou, every household would take part in the hunt, although perhaps not communally as was needed with the large caribou herds. The Vikings hunted with clubs or used nets to pull the seals out of the water, but the harpoon would have been a far more efficient way to catch seals.

Throughout their time in Greenland, the Vikings had a lean economy, with little surplus to carry people through bad years. Thus, it was highly vulnerable to changes in the environment, the main factor that contributed to the settlements' eventual demise. To be fair, though, the Greenland colonies lasted almost 500 years, and while there, the inhabitants were able to build churches, explore further west, and even follow European fashions.

Thanks to the cold conditions, a large number of textiles have been preserved at Viking sites, even entire garments such as pants and hooded tops. These personal, everyday items offer plenty of details about how people looked, and they make clear that the people did not take on the superior clothing of the Thule people but instead stuck to their own traditions. Perhaps the most significant thing these medieval clothes tell historians is that the Vikings kept up with the fashions of Europe into the mid-15th century. While Greenland was a distant outpost of Europe, it was not an entirely isolated one.

Another example of keeping up with European trends can be found in the way bodies were laid out for burial. Several churches and churchyards have been discovered, and archaeologists have examined numerous graves. One thing that has become clear is that in the earliest burials, which date to the early days of Christianity among the Norse, the arms were laid by the body's side. Later, the elbows were laid at a slight angle so the hands rested on the lower abdomen. After this, the elbows were bent at right angles so the forearms crossed each other over the abdomen. In the last stage, the arms were laid across the breast in a position of prayer. Historians believe this change was due to the evolution of theology; in the early days, the afterlife was guaranteed as long as one was baptized and buried on consecrated ground, but after the rise of the concept of Purgatory, corpses were laid out in a more pious position. The same trend has been seen in Danish and Swedish cemeteries of the same period, further hinting at regular contact between Greenland and the mainland.

The burials have also contained some surprises. In the burial ground at Herjolfsnes, a coffin was found containing a rune stick with the following inscription: "This woman, whose name was Gudveg, was laid overboard [buried] in the Greenland Sea." The coffin was not empty, however, as it contained the remnants of fatty tissue. The rest of the body had decomposed, so it was impossible to tell if this was the woman Gudveg, who may have washed ashore, or another individual. The archaeologist who excavated it theorizes that the woman was buried at sea and then ceremonially "reburied" in consecrated earth in the grave of another person, perhaps her husband, via the use of a rune stick.

At Thjodhild's Church, one of the earliest churches built in Greenland, archaeologists have found a mass grave containing the skeletons of 13 men and a child around the age of 9. The bones were disarticulated, showing that they had been deposited as bare bones, and the skulls were lined up on one end. Three of the adult skulls had fatal injuries inflicted by a sharp instrument, perhaps an axe or a sword. Another skeleton had an older cut wound that had healed. Was this mass grave the result of a feud? If so, it must have happened in some remote spot and the bodies, when recovered, had lost their flesh and were transported in a jumble to the churchyard. Another single grave in the same churchyard had a knife stuck between the ribs, an even more explicit proof of violence.

A reconstruction of Thjódhild's Chapel at Brattahlid, Greenland

19th century picture of the ruins of a church at Hvalsey, Greenland

While the Vikings in Greenland were mostly self-sufficient, they did maintain contact with the outside world. The *King's Mirror*, a Norwegian text written in the mid 13th century, explained, "It happens in Greenland … that all that is taken there from other countries is costly there, because the country lies so far from other countries that people rarely travel there. Every item, with which they might help the country, they must buy from other countries, both iron and all the timber with which they build houses. People export these goods from there: goatskins, ox-hides, sealskins and the rope … which they cut out of the fish called walrus and which is called skin rope, and their tusks … The people have been christened, and have both churches and priests."

This account is confirmed in another source. In a letter dated to 1282, Pope Martin IV wrote to Archbishop Jon of Nidaros in Norway that church tithes from Greenland were paid in hides, sealskins, walrus tusks, and rope made from walrus hide. The pope instructed that these tithes should be converted into silver and gold. It's interesting to note that these tithes were specifically to help out with the Crusades, a truly international effort at reestablishing Christian rule in the Holy Land. It is unclear if the pope realized that Greenland's settlers had no precious metals and that it fell on the Norwegians to make the exchange. This apparently did not happen, because the next surviving record of the tithes, from 1327, indicates that it was still paid in ivory.

Ivory and walrus skin rope were the most valuable exports. Walrus and narwhal ivory were unique to Greenland, and walrus skin rope was the strongest available and in high demand for use on ships. Other rarities such as polar bear skins and live falcons were also exported. These exports were so valuable that some historians have calculated that the tithes from Greenland were worth more than those from Iceland, a far more populous land.

Ivory was in high demand and short supply during the earlier period of the Greenland settlements. Royal and ecclesiastical courts used it for jewelry, gaming pieces, crosses, boxes, and other luxury items, but the supply of elephant ivory had been cut off by the Muslim conquests of the Middle East and North Africa. This situation changed after the conquest of the Holy Land by the Crusaders, and by the 14th century, elephant ivory imports were on the rise. Ivory went out of fashion the following century, perhaps because it had lost its novelty, and the loss of value of one of its greatest exports must have been a severe blow to Greenland's economy. Trade seems to have dropped sharply around this time, and the last record of ships returning from a trading expedition to Greenland was in 1410.

Ivory and walrus hide was sought in the rich hunting grounds of Nordsetur, up the western coast in Disko Bay and other points north. This was a hazardous trip along a rough and barren coastline, and there were are numerous accounts of hunting parties getting caught by the weather and freezing to death. The rewards were worth the risk, however, so hunting parties departed every year. The *Grønlands Historiske Mindesmaerker*, a collection of accounts from Greenland, claimed that "all Greenlandic farmers of a high rank had large ships and vessels built to send these on hunting trips in the northern settlements and were equipped with all kinds of hunting implements and trimmed timber, and sometimes they even participated … These so-called Nordsetur men had their booths or huts in Greipar and some in Krogsfjordshede."

Scholars believe these locations were at around 67 degrees North latitude, a little south of Disko Bay, but this wasn't the extent of the Vikings' travels. In fact, the only archaeological evidence for occupation was a little to the north of this, at the western point of the Nuussuaq Peninsula (74 degrees North). This small building is thought to have been used to store walrus and narwhal tusks.

There are about 200 runic inscriptions from Greenland, most consisting of just a single name or a terse line, offering tantalizing glimpses into the past that present more questions than answers. For example, a runestone was found on the island of Kingiktorssuaq at 73 degrees north, made of local materials and found atop a cairn, one of three set atop a mountain. It reads, "Erlingur Sigvarsson, Bjarni Thordarson, and Enridi Oddsson built Saturday before Rogation Day a cairn." Why they built a cairn at such a remote place is unknown, but they did gain a small measure of immortality.

They also caused no small amount of puzzlement among historians. The date on the inscription sets its creation in late April, when the sea in this area is still covered in ice. This means they either wintered over, in which case the cairn may have been a signal for help, or they may have traveled overland on dog sleds, relying on a Thule technology that all other evidence found to date indicates the Vikings never used.

Further north, some Viking artifacts have been found in Thule culture dwellings dating to the 13th and 14th centuries, including iron blades and fragments of chainmail. Their presence does not necessarily mean the Vikings came this far north, since they may have been products of trade or scavenged from a shipwreck. That it might have been traded is hinted at by finds in the Western Settlement of musk ox hair, an animal that was only found on the far northern fringes of Greenland. Excavations at the Western Settlement have also yielded meteoric iron from the Cape York meteor field at 76 degrees north, which is interesting because it was previously thought that the Vikings got all their iron from Iceland.

Other finds include fragments of bronze pots of a style made in Europe in the late 13th century, discovered in houses dating to that time in far northern Greenland and on Devon Island in Canada. Fragments of bronze church bells have also been found in native dwellings, although it is unclear how they would have used them other than for scrap metal or as curiosities.

Another odd legacy of these hunting trips was uncovered by the bishop's church at Gardar. Buried in the churchyard were rows of walrus skulls. Some narwhal skulls were buried in the eastern part of the chancel. Why this was done remains a mystery.

The King's Mirror is correct in asserting that a wide variety of everyday goods was brought to Greenland. Even humble clay vessels, a common item in any medieval home, had to be shipped from Norway for lack of local clay.

Most of the trade was conducted by Norwegian and Icelandic merchants. The inhabitants of Greenland did not have many seagoing vessels, only smaller ships with which to hug the coast. This was also the case in Iceland, where a scarcity of wood meant that no shipbuilding industry could develop.

Religion

The *Saga of Erik the Red* states that Leif the Lucky introduced Christianity to Greenland around the year 1001, around the same time that Iceland converted. His father, Erik the Red, remained a pagan for most of his life, but his mother Thjódhild became an ardent convert and built a church at their farm at Brattahlid. The saga mentions the amusing detail that Thjódhild built the church far enough away from the house that her husband wouldn't be annoyed by the services.

The location of Erik the Red's farm is known, and in 1961 archaeologists uncovered the remains of a small church on the land. While it's impossible to say for sure that this is the church that Thjódhild built, it remains an intriguing possibility. The interior measured just 7 x 11 feet, with thick turf walls lined with wood on the inside. Low benches were found inside, and the churchyard had 144 burials. Radiocarbon dating of the bones show that the people had been buried from the end of the 10th century to the end of the 12th century. These earliest dates, and the building's construction style, correspond to the time when Greenland was first settled. Since the *Book of the Icelanders* states that the first settlement of Greenland happened 14 or 15 winters before Iceland accepted Christianity, which would date the settlement to about 985, it raises the possibility that at least some Greenlanders were already Christian when they arrived.

The Tale of the Greenlanders recounts that one of the neighbors of the new church, Sokki Thorisson, convinced the other farmers that Greenland should have a bishop. Sokki's son Einar made the journey to King Sigurd Jorsalfar of Norway to make the request, bringing as gifts a pile of walrus tusks, skins, and a live polar bear. How Einar managed to get the bear onto a boat and keep both himself and the beast alive all the way to Norway was not described, but the king was duly impressed by these gifts and he appointed the Norwegian priest Arnald as bishop in 1124. From then on, Greenland had a series of bishops.

The next recorded visit was by Bishop Helgi in 1210 or 1212. After that, there was a resident bishop, although at times the man would spend long periods away in Iceland or Norway. The last bishop to live in Greenland was Bishop Alf, who died in 1378. By that time the settlements were declining, and it seems the church authorities did not think it important enough to assign another bishop. None of the bishops were from Greenland, having instead come either from Norway or from leading Icelandic families.

The bishop had his seat at Gardar in the Eastern Settlement, modern Igaliku, where there was a large stone church and an extensive farm, the biggest in Greenland. Its stables had space for as many as 150 cattle, while that of a typical chieftain would have had only 20 or 30 and a smallholder would have had only two to five. As this indicates, the bishops seem to have been reasonably well funded. The church measured 35 x 19 yards, a respectable size for a church even on mainland Europe, and had a nave, a narrow chancel, and two side chapels. Like many medieval churches, it was added to and rebuilt, with the most recent rebuilding coming in the 13th century. Traces of two earlier churches can still be found, and remains of stained glass windows and bronze church bells have been found.

In a grave in the northern part of the chapel at Gardar, a gold ring and a beautiful crozier made of walrus ivory were recovered. The skeleton was radiocarbon dated to between 1223 and 1290, which means this bishop was most likely Olaf, who died in 1280 or 1281. His predecessor Nikolas died in 1240, and Nikolas's predecessor Helgi died in 1230. No other bishop died in Greenland within the radiocarbon dating's statistical range.

A total of 17 churches have been found in the Eastern Settlement, along with two or three in the Western Settlement. The more scattered and less understood Middle Settlement has yet to produce any churches, but that is most likely due to the lack of extensive excavations in the area. It's quite clear from the number of churches for such a relatively small population that religion played a central role in the settlers' lives. Some of the churches were quite large and fitted with luxurious items such as glass windows, leaving plenty of people to wonder whether the resources could have been better spent trying to keep the colonies flourishing.

Most churches were quite small and built of a combination of turf and stone. Only two remain today that were built entirely of stone. Both of these are well preserved and can be visited by hardy travelers.

In addition to regular churches and the see at Gardar, archaeologists have found what they believe to be a monastery and associated church at Narsarsuaq. If their interpretation is correct, this would be the westernmost monastery in medieval times.

Like in Iceland, many of these churches were privately built by prosperous local farmers who would then have some say over how the tithes were spent. The bishop had final say over the rights of the various churches; for example, not all churches had the right to run baptisms or burials, which involved fees. As a result, there was a struggle between the bishop and the farmers who erected churches as to who would have what income streams and who controlled them. The church eventually won this struggle in Iceland in 1297, but it is unclear what happened in Greenland. Norwegian law eradicated the rights of private churches, and Greenland had accepted direct Norwegian rule in 1261, but it is not clear from available evidence whether this edict was ever enforced.

The settlements were quite spread out, so a shortage of priests was an enduring problem for the Christians in Greenland. Bread and wine for the Eucharist was scarce, and on one occasion a priest wrote to his superior asking if something else could be used instead. The answer, however, was no. It was also common to bury people with a pole stuck from the surface down to the person's chest. When a priest finally came through the district, he would pull up the pole, pour some holy water down on the body, and give the person last rites.

Surviving Literature

In addition to the archaeology and Icelandic sagas that tell the story of the Vikings in Greenland, a few pieces of literature created in Greenland were preserved in Iceland during its high point of recording old sagas and tales in the 13th-15th centuries. Others referred to Greenland but were created elsewhere. There are also the memories of the Inuit, the descendants of the Thule people with whom the Vikings interacted.

All of these stories started off in the oral tradition and were only later written down. While the passage of time no doubt brought changes, the stories are invaluable for understanding the past.

An early tale is the *Saga of the People of Floi*. It tells the story of the Icelander Thorgils Scar-legs, who in the winter of 998-999 or 999-1000 sailed to Greenland to visit his friend Erik the Red. Having never made the journey before, he put it off until too late in the season and was forced to land in eastern Greenland. Some of his crew mutinied, stole his ship, and sailed off. Thorgils and the remaining crewmembers toughed it out for a time and eventually met some natives, a man and three women. They would have been from the Dorset, a group that hunted at that time in eastern Greenland. The Vikings attacked them, wounding them and driving them away.

Later on, Thorgils and his men built a skin boat and sailed south, hoping to skirt the coast and find Erik's settlement. On the way they ran into some more natives, but this time they got along. The natives borrowed their boat and brought it back. Thorgils and his men continued their journey, and after a few days they made it to the Eastern Settlement.

Two other Norse sagas, found in the *Poetic Edda*, are *The Lay of Atli* and *The Ballad of Atli*. The first dates to the early 11th century, and the second is from the latter half of the 11th century. The *Ballad* is essentially an extended version of the *Lay*.

The *Ballad* is difficult to summarize because there are missing passages and translators have struggled with many Old Norse words that appear nowhere else. The scribe who initially wrote them down in medieval Iceland noted they were from Greenland, and this is backed up by the appearance of a polar bear in a dream sequence. Also, the largest warrior band mentioned in the tale only managed to gather together 30 men.

What follows is a wild and bloody tale even by Norse standards. The chieftain, Atli, is married to Guthrum, and when Guthrum's two brothers visit, they quarrel and Atli kills them. Guthrum then avenges her brothers' death by cooking her and Atli's two sons and serving them to the chieftain. Once he finishes the meal, she tells him what he really ate. Then she gets an assassin to kill him, and Guthrum lives into old age with the shame of what she has done. Amidst all this are prophetic dreams and the reading of runes that tell of dire futures.

A remarkable aspect of the stories of Atli is that they are Nordic versions of Burgundian tales about Attila the Hun. The Burgundians were a Germanic tribe that clashed with the Romans and eventually settled in what is now southeastern France. They had a vibrant literature that was imitated in many local versions across Europe, and finding derivations of their stories in Greenland demonstrates that even though there was no direct contact, Europe was quite interconnected in the Middle Ages.

Inuit tales, passed down from their Thule ancestors, tell many variations of the first contact with Vikings. Some stories describe simple curiosity, but in others, there was fear. One tale tells of how a Thule girl was out fetching a pail of water when she saw something red reflected in the water. Unsure what it was, she turned around and saw it was a group of Vikings. It's unclear whether the red was from their hair (which the black-haired Thule people would have never seen before) or red garments, but Inuit drawings used to illustrate these stories often show the Viking settlers wearing red clothing. In any case, the girl was terrified, dropped the pail, and ran home as quickly as she could.

In another story, a Thule man paddled his kayak into Iminguit Bay and spotted a Viking tent. He snuck up and heard the men laughing and joking inside. Deciding to play a trick on them, he struck the sides of the tent several times. The Vikings fell silent. He continued striking the tent, having fun at the their expense, but when he finally peeked inside, he found they had all died of fright.

One widely known tale, still taught in Greenland's schools, tells of how the Thule and the Vikings were at first friends but fell into conflict. It recounts how the Thule people initially discovered the Vikings living near present-day Nuuk (the Western Settlement). They were astonished by the stone houses and strange appearance of these people, as were the Vikings with them. The sides were not hostile, and the Thule began to visit frequently. Eventually, the two groups learned to communicate.

After that, there were many friendships among the two cultures, and none was closer than the friendship between two young men who hunted together, ate together, and explored the wilderness together. Like young men of all cultures, they liked to compete with one another, but they were too evenly matched. No matter what they did, they would always end up with a tie.

Eventually the Viking grew tired of this and offered a final competition. He took his Thule friend to a small island overlooked by a mountain with a sheer cliff facing in the direction of the island. There, the Viking spread out a caribou skin and said, "We'll go to the top of that mountain and fire at this target. Whoever misses gets pushed off the cliff." The Thule man wanted no part of it, but his friend insisted. At last, the Viking chiefs said that whatever happened, they wouldn't blame the Thule man or his people, because it had been the Viking's idea. With that, he relented.

The pair went up to the top of the mountain, followed by a large crowd. The Thule man fired first and hit the target. Then the Viking fired, but he missed. Accepting defeat, the Viking walked willingly to the edge of the cliff and his friend pushed him off. The mountain was named Pisissarfik, "Archer's Mountain." As the Viking chiefs promised, peace continued between the two peoples.

Ultimately, however, this peace was not to last. There was a young Thule girl named Navaranaaq who worked as a servant at a Viking farm. For reasons known only to herself, she began to sow discord between the Thule and the Vikings. To her employers, she'd say, "The Greenlanders are angry at you and they're going to attack soon." To her own kind, she'd say, "The Norsemen are planning on slaughtering you."

For a time neither side believed her, but she kept at it until the Viking settlers grew concerned. They gathered together and decided that the Thule people were a threat and that they'd better attack them before they got attacked themselves. They waited until the Thule men were away hunting caribou and attacked their settlement, killing all the women and children except for one old woman who managed to hide.

When the Thule men came back, the survivor told them the grim tale. One hunter, Qasapi, organized the enraged men for revenge. He had lost his wife and only child in the attack. Qasapi and his wife had several children before but they had all died. The last child had been a healthy infant, and they had high hopes for it until the Vikings slaughtered the entire tribe. Qasapi swore vengeance.

The first thing he did was find a talented shaman to help them. Then he built an umiak that could be broken into several smaller boats. This he covered with white cloth to make it look like an iceberg. The hunters and the shaman all climbed inside and sailed up Nuuk Fjord to where the Vikings had their settlement. At first they found only abandoned buildings. They learned that the Vikings, fearing reprisals, had gathered together for protection at the chieftain Uunngortoq's homestead. Linguists believe "Uunngortoq" is an Inuit attempt to pronounce the Norse name "Yngvardur".

Qasapi and his men maneuvered the camouflaged umiak up close to the chieftain's farmhouse, where several Vikings stood outside as sentries. They didn't pay much attention to the boat, thinking it was a glacier. As the current brought the boat closer, the different sections broke apart. The Norsemen didn't think this was strange, since glaciers commonly break apart at more temperate latitudes. Qasapi then told the shaman to cast a spell to send the Norsemen inside and make them stay there. This he did, and once the coast was clear, the little boats came ashore and the war party sprang out. Qasapi crept up to the window of Uunngortoq's house and saw the Norsemen gathered inside gambling. The prize was the head of Qasapi's wife, stuck on the end of a stick. The tale says the Vikings were playing poker, which is obviously a later embellishment since poker wasn't invented until the 19th century.

Qasapi then had his men pile up fuel against the building's one door and set it on fire. Soon the building was ablaze. The Vikings, panicked and coughing, tried to burst out through the flaming door or crawl out the windows, but those who survived the flames and smoke got shot down by the Thule men's arrows.

Only the chieftain Uunngortoq managed to break free, clutching his little son to his chest. Qasapi raced after him, and they ran for a long time, with Qasapi gradually gaining on his prey. As they ran past a lake, Uunngortoq glanced over his shoulder and saw that he was losing the race. Kissing his son one last time, Uunngortoq threw him into the lake and kept on running. Now he was able to run faster and eventually outpaced Qasapi, getting away. He was never seen again.

Eventually, the Thule people learned that the girl Navaranaaq had been telling lies. Enraged that they had been fooled into a war with their friends, they tied a rope to her hair and dragged her along the ground, asking her, "Navaranaaq, are you happy now?" Each time they asked, she'd reply, "You better believe I am." They dragged her so long that they wore away her back, and then they killed her without using any weapons, a slow death reserved for the worst criminals. By then, however, the Vikings never again lived among the Nuuk fjords. The Western Settlement was dead.

There are several variations of this story, and in one Qasapi catches up with Uunngortoq. Since the Viking had cut off the arm of Qasapi's brother, Qasapi cut off Uunngortoq's arm. Holding it aloft, he shouted, "As long as I live, and as long as you live, your arm will not be forgotten!"

Another tale tells of a different fate for the Eastern Settlement. It says the Thule and the Vikings lived in peace. One day, three ships sailed up the fjord and attacked the Viking settlement. It turned out they were pirates. The settlers managed to drive them away, but they feared that more pirates would come, so they asked the Thule to take the Viking women and children with them up the fjord to safety. This they did. After some time, the Thule returned to the settlement, only to find it destroyed by the pirates. As a result, the Viking women and children joined their tribe, marrying into it and becoming assimilated into their culture.

It must be said that there is no archaeological or DNA evidence for this, but the tale is significant in that it shows the two peoples living in peace. The mention of pirates is interesting because the Thule had no equivalent in their culture, so they must have learned about pirates, and the fear of being attacked by them, from the Vikings.

Another tantalizing tale centers around Sisimiut Fjord at Ikereteq. A spot there is quite green, a sign that there are ruins beneath. The local name, Qallunaannguit, seems to bear that out, as it translates to "the dear pale ones." The local Inuit still tell a tale that a Viking family lived there. The man was a great hunter who used a harpoon and hunted in the Thule style. On the other bank of the fjord is another ruin said to have been the home of a Thule family. The man of that house was also a great hunter. The pair became close friends, and if one got a good catch, they would share it with the other.

This story is interesting in that it has obvious parallels to the tale of the two archers, albeit with a happier ending. Even more important, it tells of a Viking family that adopted Thule culture in order to survive. Perhaps this great hunter was one of the last of the settlers, and he finally decided to give up the failed way of life to live in the Thule fashion. Near the end, it must have been obvious to even the most stubborn Viking settlers that the Thule were thriving in the same spots where they struggled.

Cultural Contacts

As the stories told by both sides suggest, there was plenty of interaction between the Vikings and Thule. When Denmark, which claimed the North Atlantic islands once owned by Norway via a political union, decided to recolonize Greenland in 1721, they expected to find the descendants of the Viking settlers still there, ready for conversion from Catholicism to Lutheranism. Instead they found the Inuit, a native people who still had memories of the Vikings.

When the Vikings first arrived in Greenland, they found the remains of human habitation. These were no doubt from the culture archaeologists call Paleo-Eskimo, which had abandoned the area several centuries earlier. For a time, the settlers would be alone in southern Greenland, but all that changed when they came in contact with the Thule people, ancestors to the modern Inuit.

The Thule people, who had arrived in northwestern Greenland in the 12th century from Canada, steadily moved down the coast. In 1266, they were said to have lived on an island some distance north of the Western Settlement. By about 1300, they appear to have settled the outer fjords of the Western Settlement, close to the Vikings' seasonal seal hunting grounds. Perhaps the two cultures came into conflict over hunting rights. Thule sites show an increasing number of Norse artifacts, either traded or scavenged. Interestingly, some bits of metal were sharpened and reused for the tips of harpoons, a technology the Vikings never adopted themselves.

Did the two peoples get along? As the aforementioned tales indicate, oral tradition has it that the Thule people attacked and destroyed the Western Settlement, but this has been disputed because there is no material evidence for it. The *Icelandic Annals* mention another attack in 1379, during which the Thule killed 18 people and made slaves of two boys. It does not mention where, but since communication with the Western Settlement had apparently ceased by this point, it probably occurred in the Middle Settlement or Eastern Settlement.

Thule culture had heartily adapted to the environment, using dogsleds to travel quickly on land and large skin boats called umiaks that allowed them to hunt whales. They replaced the earlier Dorset people, who had neither of these things and who primarily hunted walrus. The Dorset were soon absorbed by the Thule people or moved away, but it appears that the earliest contact between Vikings and natives might have been between the early settlers and the Dorset. This would explain why the settlers met the "skraelings" ("weaklings", as they called the natives) before experiencing a lull in contact between 1200 and 1300. This lull might have caused by the departure of the Dorset people before the arrival of the Thule people.

The southern migration continued, and by the 14th century, the Thule occupied the outer parts of the fjords in southwestern Greenland, spots vital to Norse subsistence. As the weather grew colder in the Little Ice Age, the Vikings lost their adaptive edge. They had relied on dairy farming, a hazardous prospect in Greenland in the best of times, and this soon became impossible. In addition, their boats were less maneuverable in narrow fjords choked with ice floes than the Thule boats, and the Thule craft were much more easily handled when being dragged over pack ice.

It appears that the two groups stayed more or less separate other than for trading and perhaps raiding. There are few accounts in Thule or Norse folklore of cohabitation, and neither side adopted any important cultural traits from the other. It appears that the Vikings did not learn much from their neighbors, since they continued to use their woolen clothing despite the sealskin clothes of the Thule people being far better adapted for the climate. They also failed to take on the Thule people's boating and hunting technology.

Several genetic tests have been conducted over the years searching for traces of Norse ethnicity among the Inuit people, who are descended from the Thule and thus should have carried any genetic markers from any mixing. None has been found. The only Scandinavian genes to have made it into the Inuit gene pool came during the later wave of colonization by Denmark starting in the 18th century.

Some of the few hints at a mixing of the cultures came from Inuit sites after 1500, where wooden buckets and ladles have been found. These were common in Norse homes and stored food, were used in cheese making, and stored urine used for bleaching and dying wool. It appears the Inuit appropriated the use of this object from the last surviving settlers.

If there was any significant amount of trading between the Thule people, the Vikings no doubt traded for raw materials such as ivory that would have been turned into artifacts or exported. The church may also have played a hand in limiting contact; Catholics strongly feared heretics, especially as criticism of the dominant ideology began to grow on mainland Europe. Church leaders may have looked warily at the Thule, who were so culturally and ethnically different and had distinctive polytheistic and shamanistic traditions.

The Thule, on the other hand, showed an interest in Norse objects. Some 170 Norse artifacts have been found at Thule sites, such as shears, knife blades, and even chess pieces. Some of the later finds may have been scavenged from abandoned sites, but the rest are no doubt the product of trade. There is also a similar number of ornamental bone pins found nowhere else in the Thule culture area that look like a medieval stylus, or writing tool. These appear to be a Thule imitation of a Norse artifact.

Norse artifacts were widely traded. Some have been found as far north as 83 degrees North on the northeastern coast of Greenland, diagonally opposite from the Norse settlement area. The majority of the artifacts are made of metal, which the Thule culture rarely worked themselves.

Then there is an enigmatic ivory Thule carving from southern Baffin Island dating to the 13th or 14th century. It shows a hooded figure wearing a cloak that is split about a third of the way up the front. A cross is carved on the chest, either intended to depict a cross hanging from the neck or emblazoned on the garment itself. The clothing looks unlike anything the Inuit wore, and the cross is a giveaway that this is depicting a Viking. The style of robe fits with the fashion of the time, and it is quite different from those carved by the Thule in Greenland that appear to depict

Vikings in European clothing. Thus, experts assume it was a local product.

Hans Egede, the Lutheran minister in charge of recolonizing Greenland, explored many of the Viking ruins and spoke extensively with the Inuit, who called themselves Kalals. He reported that the Kalals "often had wars with the Norwegians." This is odd since there is little hard evidence for this. Perhaps this was his interpretation of an account he heard in a language he struggled to learn. He also learned that the Kalals made use of the Viking houses as shelters.

The term "Kalal" itself is of interest, because Poul Egede, Hans Egede's son, noted that the natives "say the appellation was introduced by the old Christians who earlier lived in their country." Some scholars believe it comes from the Icelandic word "klaedast", meaning "skin", signifying those who wear skin clothing. Kalal was used as a term of designation only by those Inuit living in the south, near where the Eastern Settlement once stood. Perhaps these southern Inuit remembered contact with the largest colony, because throughout the rest of Greenland, even in Egede's time, the Inuit referred to themselves as Inuit.

Linguists have also found a few other Inuit words with possible Norse origins. The term "skraeling", meaning "weakling", is only found in Norse sources. Its first mention comes from the *Historia Norvegiae* ("*History of Norway*") from the late 11th century, which relates, "On the other side of Greenland, toward the north, hunters have found some little people whom they call Skraelings; their situation is that when they are hurt by weapons their sores become white without bleeding, but when they are mortally wounded their blood will hardly stop running. They have no iron at all; they use missiles made of walrus tusks and sharp stones for knives."

It's noteworthy that at this early stage, these people were not found further south, even as the *Book of the Icelanders* mentions remnants of their dwellings to the south. It appears that at this time the native people preferred staying up north where game was plentiful. It was only with the drop in temperatures during the Little Ice Age that the Thule/Inuit would begin to move south.

Traveling Further West

Greenland was a stepping stone to exploration further west. The Norse, ever hungry for more land and further exploration, would have been convinced that something more lay to the west. Driftwood on the western shore, as well as the behavior of sea birds, would have hinted at lands beyond the horizon, so it would have not taken long before they checked out the area for themselves.

Leif Erikson explored the east coast of North America around the year 1000, landing at three places. The first he called Helluland ("Land of Flat Rocks"), describing it in a way that makes it sound like Baffin Island. It was a quick journey due west from the Nordsetur hunting huts located at Greipar (67 degrees North) and Krogsfjordshede in northern Disko Bay (70 degrees North). The next stop was Markland ("Forest Land"), most likely Labrador, and then Vinland

("Wine Land"), which probably corresponds to Newfoundland and other points south.

Christian Krohg's painting, *Leiv Eiriksson discovers North America*

Wes Gill's picture of Baffin Island, a place some believe may have been settled by Vikings

It was on the northern tip of Newfoundland near L'Anse aux Meadows that archaeologists uncovered a small Viking settlement. It has all the characteristics of a base for further exploration inland, and archaeologists are continuing the search for more evidence of Viking settlement in North America.

Dylan Kereluk's picture of the recreated Viking settlement at L'Anse aux Meadows

Gordon E. Robertson's picture of a recreated Long House at L'Anse aux Meadows,

Newfoundland

Native sites in the far north of Canada have artifacts of Norse origin. These include fragments of worked iron and bronze, bits of chainmail, cloth of Norse manufacture, and even a portion of a bronze balance. This last item, used by the Norse to weigh objects that were going to be traded, was found on the western coast of Ellesmere Island, 1,250 miles from the Western Settlement. It's unclear whether the Vikings came and traded there, or if the native people traded the object, with the balance moving along Arctic trade route and ending up so far from its point of origin.

The southernmost Norse artifact in North America is a coin uncovered in Maine at the Goddard site, a Late Ceramic period site with two radiocarbon dates showing activity in 1180 and 1235. Dubbed the "Maine Penny," it is a Norwegian penny minted between 1065 and 1080. How it got there is hinted at by other finds at the Goddard site; some of the tools were made from chalcedonies from the Bay of Fundy region of Nova Scotia, and Ramah chert from northern Labrador. There was also a tool of Dorset origin. Historians thus believe there was an active trade among people in the region, and the penny likely came down as part of this trade route. The coin was perforated, so it may have been worn as a pendant.

Back in Greenland, there is indirect evidence of long-term contact. Most of the wooden artifacts found in Viking sites in Greenland do not have the little holes made by shipworms characteristic of driftwood. Since there are no sources of wood in Greenland or Iceland, the wood must have come from either Markland or Norway via Iceland. However, since Iceland would almost certainly have used all wood imported from Norway or raised the price accordingly, the closer and easier source would be Markland.

Another tantalizing clue is that among the fibers of Greenland textiles, which are mostly made of sheep's wool, occasionally fibers from other animals are found. This included brown bear and bison, neither of which have ever lived on Greenland. While these could be from the Scandinavian brown bear and the European bison, a closer source lies in North America.

While some of the evidence indicates there was trade among the Vikings and natives in Greenland and North America, there is no written record describing trade in North America.

The Decline of the Greenland Settlements

It has long been a matter of debate just how the Viking colonies in Greenland died out. One old theory is that they were wiped out by hostile Thule, but while there is some mention of hostilities between the Thule and Vikings in the traditions of both, there is no evidence that the settlers were massacred. Instead, researchers have focused on the change of climate. When Erik the Red first came to Greenland, the region was enjoying a period of mild weather. Starting around 1300, however, there was a 500-year drop in temperatures, now known as the Little Ice Age. Studying 14th century data from ice cores, scientists discovered that there was a string of cold years from

1308-1318, 1324-1329, 1343-1362, and 1380-1384.

This would have caused a host of problems. The inland glaciers grew in size and moved closer to the settlements, and during summer melting, more water would rush down the rivers. Where once the rivers had flowed clear, now they were bloated and sandy, which made it harder and worse to drink. Flooding would have also left sandy deposits on pastures, which inhibited the growth of the grass that was already struggling because of the shorter, cooler summers.

Icelandic records show sea ice reaching Iceland in 1306, 1319-1321, 1350, and 1374, as well as many years in the 15th century. This would have impeded shipping and trade, and Greenland was no doubt even harder hit.

The Norse were dependent on the summers to give them enough forage to support the animals that in turn supported them. While they could survive a poor summer or two, the 20 bad summers in a row they endured in the mid-14th century was likely the death blow to the Western Settlement and must have seriously constrained the Middle Settlement and Eastern Settlement as well.

The excavation of a farm at Nipaatsoq at the Western Settlement tells a grim tale. Cut marks on cow bones show that the settlers ate their cattle, even going so far as to boil their hooves. This was an act of desperation, feeding the hungry at the expense of their future. It was also illegal under Norse law. The fodder must have run out. After this, they ate their dogs.

In the farmhouse, there was also evidence that the firewood ran out. A species of fly that can only survive in warm temperatures disappeared, replaced by two species of flies that are tolerant to cold temperatures. These cold-weather flies are generally carrion eaters, and that carrion may have been the Viking inhabitants themselves, lying dead in their failed dairy farms after the last of their food supplies had been exhausted.

Another late period farm, right next to the Farm Beneath the Sand, revealed a similar tale. The remains of a dog were found with butchering marks on the bones, indicating the inhabitants had been forced to eat an animal that would have been vital for the autumn caribou hunt. Here, too, the remains of carrion eating flies have been found in abundance.

Several other farms nearby had suffered the same fate. Collapsed wooden roof beams, valuable in this treeless land, had never been collected by the neighbors. Dog skeletons were found in the houses. All of these farms were abandoned in the middle of the 14th century. It appears that an entire parish of the Western Settlement had died out in a single harsh winter.

Not all the settlers suffered such a bad end. Most buildings were evacuated in an orderly manner, with all important possessions taken away. The inhabitants probably retreated first to the Middle Settlement and Eastern Settlement to the south, which had slightly more favorable weather, and then back to Iceland or Norway.

It must be remembered that the Little Ice Age, while on average colder, had fluctuations in temperature. Warmer years gave the hardy Vikings time to recover, and perhaps a false sense of hope that things would get better. This was not to be, however, and the cumulative effect of the poor weather and reduced trade, along with the knowledge that there were literally greener pastures elsewhere, took their inevitable toll.

It appears that the Western Settlement disappeared in the middle of the 14th century, while the Eastern Settlement petered out around 1450. When the Middle Settlement was abandoned is not clear, but logic dictates that it probably happened sometime between the other two dates. The Western Settlement, of course, would have been most vulnerable to a drop in temperatures, with ice blocking the openings to the fjords and making it difficult to go fishing or to communicate with the other settlements.

The struggles of the settlements must be seen in the wider context of troubles all across the northern zone of medieval Europe. The cooling climate caused the abandonment of upland hill farms in Scotland, first settled in the Viking Age or in the Early Middle Ages. A string of bad crops led to food riots in many northern towns, and even as far south as Flanders.

At the same time, these climatic changes should not be exaggerated. They occurred gradually over time, leaving each generation a bit poorer than the one previous. Medieval people were accustomed to hard winters and an occasional lean year, and with a lack of long-term records of temperature and soil loss, they would not have been fully aware of the extent of their decline until a series of disastrous winters led to the apparently rapid abandonment of the Western Settlement. Perhaps those in the Eastern Settlement fooled themselves into thinking that their land, which had always been superior to that of their northern neighbors, would continue to support them. For a time it likely did, but the inevitable end was coming for them too.

Other theories have been proposed for the abandonment of Greenland. Some maintain that the fights with the Thule were more dramatic than the archaeological record attests. Others point to the Black Death, which was ravaging Europe near the end of the settlement period. The disease did not have to even make it to Greenland for it to hurt the colony, as the loss of a third of Europe's population might have disrupted the tenuous, long-distance trade with these outposts. Also, with the loss of so many people in Scandinavia and Iceland to the plague, a large amount of farmland would have been freed up, meaning Greenland's inhabitants might have found the prospect of farming in a milder climate preferable to staying in Greenland.

Whatever the reasons, contact between Greenland and Norway waned in the 14th century. Sometimes years would go by without a single ship arriving. Since it was a Crown colony, only royal ships could trade there, and these ships were generally reserved for more important regions. When the Black Death hit Norway in 1349, it exacerbated an already existing trend. On top of that, the Hanseatic League crippled Norway as a sea power, and contact with Greenland all but dried up. The last landfall mentioned in the *Icelandic Annals* was in 1406, when a ship headed from Norway to Iceland was blown off course. A letter written around 1492 by Pope Alexander VI (the infamous Rodrigo Borgia) claimed that the freezing of the sea had kept any ship from visiting Greenland for 80 years.

Greenland did not have a very large population, and when people began to emigrate, it would have caused a serious domino effect, making the population as a whole less genetically viable and perhaps encouraging more emigration. For the young, this meant fewer potential partners of marriageable age. Young men may have chosen to find their fortunes elsewhere, while young women may have tried to find a husband in a better place. Indeed, excavations of late settlements in Greenland have shown that young women are underrepresented in the burials, hinting that they did leave. It would have been harder for young men to leave since they would have had herds and homes to tend and eventually inherit. Nevertheless, it's apparent that some did, no matter what the personal cost was.

This demographic shift, combined with the poorer weather, may have led to a dramatic reduction in population in just a generation or two. One mystery is why this emigration is not mentioned in any records. Perhaps it took place too steadily for people to truly notice. The population of Iceland during this period was around 40,000-70,000, so a few dozen people returning from Greenland every year would not have been worthy of note. Indeed, it might be anachronistic to look at Greenland as a separate entity, especially since the Icelandic texts do not make it out to be. To contemporary Norsemen, Greenland was simply an extension of the habitable lands in the North Atlantic.

The plague also affected trade. The port of Bergen, the main connection to Greenland, was ravaged by the plague, and this greatly reduced the number of ships leaving the harbor every year. Less profitable runs, such as that to faraway Greenland, dropped in frequency. This would have been yet another factor in making the colony seem more isolated and unattractive. Newly available lands in Iceland would have seemed that much more tempting.

An interesting study of human and animal bones in Greenland's settlements suggests a change in diet. In the early years of the colonies, the inhabitants' diet included only about 20-30% seafood, whether fish or seal. By the 14th century, however, seal meat made up 50-80% of their diet. This was due to a scaling back of livestock. Cattle, the staple of the early settlers, all but vanished by 1300, replaced with sheep and goats. These smaller animals were better able to deal with the limited fodder and rough weather, but they obviously provided less meat and cheese.

The earliest settlements even show evidence of pigs, which were entirely unsuited to Greenland. This is further proof the initial settlers were overly optimistic about the potential of their new lands. Pigs are quite bad for the soil since they root around in it, and that would have caused much erosion in the early days before the settlers got rid of them. The same story played out in Iceland, where pigs were probably a major factor in the destruction of the fragile birch forests the first settlers found clinging to the thin topsoil there.

Another favored animal that proved unsuitable to life in Greenland was the horse. A few horse bones have been found, proof that the Vikings did try to bring them there, but its high usage of forage and an aversion to eating them meant they were impractical. The rough terrain, frequently broken by fjords and streams, left few places to ride them, and their use quickly died out.

Interestingly, for much of the time the settlements survived in Greenland, the human bones show that the settlers were no more prone to disease than their fellow Norsemen in Scandinavia, indicating that they were not any more malnourished than the average medieval farmer.

Altogether, the decline of the Vikings in Greenland remains a murky picture. A recent study on the medieval climate has challenged the traditional idea that the Little Ice Age killed off the colonies; instead, it suggests that the Medieval Warm Period, which ran from the 10th-14th centuries, did not affect all areas of the North Atlantic. Studies of the isotopes of boulders in Greenland and Baffin Island show that the weather was no warmer during this period than usual. The isotopes indicate when the boulders were deposited by glaciers, thus indicating the southern edge of glaciations, and the results show that glaciers were as far south at the beginning of the Viking period of settlement as they were at the end. If this study is correct, it was consistently cold throughout the settlement period. This flies in the face of archaeological and textual evidence, and the study remains controversial.

The last written record of the Greenland colonies comes from the Eastern Settlement, where a brief note dated to 1408 mentions a wedding in Hvalsey Church, in the fjord of the same name. It also mentions a less happy event: the burning to death of a man named Kolbein on the charge of witchcraft a few years earlier.

The marriage was between Sigrid Bjornsdottir and Thorstein Olafsson, and the marriage certificate was drawn up the following year at Gardar and ended up in Iceland, where the couple had moved. Two letters related to the wedding also survive. These, dated to 1414 and 1424, are both witness statements swearing that they had been present at the wedding. A total of four witnesses, all now living in Iceland, signed these letters. It is unclear from the letters why the wedding needed to be witnessed, but historians figure it may have been about potential inheritance. What is interesting is that the couple and all four witnesses had been living in Greenland and moved to Iceland, a potentially representative example of the exodus.

Hvalsey Church still stands on a grassy hillside near the water. Its roof is long gone, but the walls stand to nearly their original height. For generations, this church fed the spiritual needs of the Eastern Settlement. It is unknown if there were any other weddings after 1408, or any baptisms or other religious services. It's only natural to wonder what the bride and groom thought as they made their vows in the church, knowing their previous way of life was coming to an end.

Online Resources

Other books about medieval history by Charles River Editors

Other books about the Vikings on Amazon

Bibliography

Barraclough, Eleanor Rosamind, Beyond the Northlands – Viking voyages and the old Norse sagas, Oxford University Press, 2016.

Brink, Stefan and Neil Price, The Viking world, Routledge, 2008.

Haywood, John, The Penguin historical atlas of the Vikings, Penguin Books, 1995.

Hjardar, Kim and Vegard Vike, Vikings at war, Casemate UK, 2016.

McCoy, Daniel, The Viking spirit – An introduction to Norse mythology and religion, 2016.

Roesdahl, Else, The Vikings, Penguin Press, 1998.

Winroth, Anders, The Age of the Vikings, Princeton University Press, 2014.

Free Books by Charles River Editors

We have brand new titles available for free most days of the week. To see which of our titles are currently free, click on this link.

Discounted Books by Charles River Editors

We have titles at a discount price of just 99 cents everyday. To see which of our titles are currently 99 cents, click on this link.

Made in United States
North Haven, CT
28 July 2023

39627995R00028